CW01082655

Original title:

Love's True Path

Copyright © 2024 Swan Charm

Author: Swan Charm

ISBN HARDBACK: 978-9916-89-121-6

ISBN PAPERBACK: 978-9916-89-122-3

ISBN EBOOK: 978-9916-89-123-0

Starlit Conversations

Under the blanket of night,
Whispers travel through the air,
Echoes of thoughts take flight,
In the glow, we share.

The Dance of Connection

Two souls spin in gentle sway,
Beneath the moon's soft gaze,
Each step a word we cannot say,
In rhythm, our hearts blaze.

Guiding Lights in the Dark

Stars twinkle above our heads,
Like dreams that light the way,
In the silence, hope spreads,
Guiding us through night to day.

Heartbeats in Harmony

In the quiet, pulses blend,
A symphony softly plays,
Each heartbeat a message we send,
Together in time, always.

Resounding Echoes in Time

In the stillness of the night,
Whispers of the past take flight.
Footsteps on a forgotten path,
Sounds of laughter, echoes of wrath.

Through the ages, voices blend,
Stories linger, never end.
Moments captured, longing sighs,
Resounding echoes in the skies.

Memories like shadows creep,
In our hearts, they gently seep.
Time may fade, but love remains,
A tapestry of joy and pains.

Every heartbeat writes a song,
Melodies where we belong.
Dancing through the hands of fate,
In the silence, we await.

So let us listen, let us hear,
The stories shared, both far and near.
In this journey, we will find,
Resounding echoes of the mind.

The Hidden Trail of Affection

In the forest, secrets lie,
Softly whispered, a gentle sigh.
Beneath the leaves, the roots go deep,
Promises made that time shall keep.

In every shadow, love will bloom,
Filling hearts, dispelling gloom.
A hidden trail we wander down,
With every step, in love we drown.

Through tangled vines, our fingers trace,
In this wild, enchanted space.
Nature hums a tender tune,
Beneath the stars, beneath the moon.

We carve our names on bark and stone,
In this land, we are not alone.
With every moment, affection grows,
In the secret garden, love flows.

Let the world outside fade away,
We'll find the words we long to say.
In this hidden haven wide,
Our hearts will wander, side by side.

The Tides of Compassion

The ocean whispers, soft and low,
Waves rise and fall, a rhythmic flow.
In the depth, our hearts align,
A bond of kindness, truly divine.

With each wave, a story told,
In the tides, compassion unfolds.
Reaching shores, where hearts embrace,
In every splash, a warm trace.

The sun sets slow, painting skies,
Mirroring love in our eyes.
Hand in hand, we navigate,
Through stormy seas, we resonate.

In the calm after the storm,
A healing touch, a heart-worn charm.
Riding waves, we learn to trust,
In compassion's tide, we find our must.

So let us sail on waters clear,
With love as our compass, drawing near.
Through the currents, we shall glide,
On the tides of compassion, we ride.

Embracing the Unknown

In shadows deep, we find our way,
With hearts unbound, to roam and stay.
Each step ahead, a whisper calls,
Through twilight's veil, our courage thralls.

The stars above, our guide anew,
In tangled paths, we'll see it through.
With every fear, we dance and soar,
The unknown waits, with open door.

Across the wild, through stormy skies,
We hold the dreams that never die.
In every breath, we claim our right,
To walk the dark, to chase the light.

Seasons of Our Affection

In spring's embrace, love starts to bloom,
With gentle whispers, dispelling gloom.
Summer's warmth, two souls entwined,
In radiant joy, our hearts aligned.

As autumn leaves begin to fall,
We gather memories, cherish all.
With shades of gold, our laughter blends,
In twilight's glow, affection extends.

Through winter's chill, we hold on tight,
In cozy nights, our love ignites.
Seasons change, yet we remain,
In every heartbeat, love's sweet refrain.

Moments Carved in Time

A fleeting glance, a soft embrace,
In stolen joy, we find our place.
Each laughter shared, a treasure found,
In simple acts, our hearts surround.

Like footprints left on shifting sand,
We weave our tales, hand in hand.
In whispers low, our secrets kept,
In dreams that linger, softly slept.

With every sunset, memories rise,
In fading light, beneath the skies.
Moments passed, yet evergreen,
In the tapestry, our lives convene.

Reflections in Still Waters

Beneath the calm, our secrets lie,
In quiet pools, where echoes sigh.
The world above, a distant dream,
In the stillness, our thoughts redeem.

Each ripple holds a story sweet,
In mirrored depths, our hearts repeat.
With every glance, we seek to find,
The threads of fate, so intertwined.

As twilight casts its golden hue,
We gaze within, and there find you.
Reflections clear, like stars at night,
In still waters, our souls take flight.

The Color of Togetherness

In shades of laughter, we find our hue,
A tapestry woven, in me and you.
With every heartbeat, a brushstroke clear,
Together we paint, forever near.

In the dawn's glow, our colors blend,
Every moment shared, a message we send.
In silence we find, a bond too bright,
The hues of our souls, in love's pure light.

Sweet Surrender

A gentle whisper, soft as a sigh,
In your warm embrace, I learn to fly.
With every surrender, a piece of me grows,
In the depth of your presence, my spirit glows.

In twilight's embrace, we let go of fear,
Finding strength in love, whenever you're near.
With sweet memories held, like stars in the night,
Surrendering softly, all feels just right.

Moments Between Breath

In the pause of silence, we find our place,
In moments between, we embrace grace.
With every heartbeat, time flows like a stream,
In the depths of stillness, we dare to dream.

As shadows dance gently on evening's edge,
We speak without words, a silent pledge.
In these fleeting seconds, love claims its space,
Forever cherished, in time's warm embrace.

The Bridge of Understanding

A bridge built with kindness, sturdy and wide,
Where hearts come together, side by side.
In every conversation, truths are revealed,
In the light of respect, our wounds are healed.

With each step taken, walls fall away,
Through laughter and tears, come what may.
In the warmth of compassion, we deeply connect,
On this bridge of understanding, we reflect.

A Tapestry of Moments

Threads of laughter, memories weave,
In the fabric of time, we believe.
Colors of joy, shadows of pain,
Each moment a stitch, a joyful refrain.

Moments like flowers, in bloom they lie,
Under the vast, embracing sky.
Each petal a story, fragrant and sweet,
A tapestry woven, where hearts meet.

Echos of whispers, gentle and clear,
Each thread a promise, drawing us near.
In the warmth of the sun, the cool of the night,
Our moments together, a guiding light.

Seasons will change, but love stays true,
In the quilt of existence, it's me and you.
Every glance shared, a fleck of gold,
In the tapestry of moments, our tale unfolds.

Resonance of Souls

In the silence, a heartbeat sings,
A connection deep, with unseen strings.
Two souls entwined, a dance so rare,
In the universe, a gentle care.

Whispers echo, beyond the time,
Notes of love, in perfect rhyme.
In the stillness, our spirits glow,
Resonance of souls, a soft flow.

Through storms we wander, hand in hand,
Together stronger, we make our stand.
Every challenge faced, every dream bold,
A story of courage, waiting to be told.

In the twilight, where shadows blend,
The light of our hearts, a constant friend.
With every heartbeat, our truth defined,
In the resonance of souls, our lives aligned.

Whispers in the Heart

In the quiet, a soft voice calls,
Whispers in the heart, as silence falls.
With every flutter, hopes take flight,
Guiding us through the darkest night.

Tender echoes, secrets shared,
In the depth of love, souls laid bare.
Soft sighs and dreams, a gentle art,
Painting the walls of the yearning heart.

Through the valleys and peaks we roam,
In the whispers, we found a home.
Each heartbeat a promise, each glance a word,
In the still of the night, our love is heard.

With every pulse, our story flows,
A river of emotions, where passion grows.
In the tapestry of time, we'll never part,
Forever entwined, whispers in the heart.

The Journey of Two Souls

On a path unknown, hand in hand,
The journey unfolds, a life unplanned.
With every step, the world ignites,
The journey of two souls, hearts take flight.

Through valleys low and mountains high,
Together we laugh, together we cry.
In the dance of time, we find our way,
Guided by love, come what may.

Stars above and the moonlight's glow,
Illuminate the paths we'll go.
With every heartbeat, a promise we keep,
In the journey of two souls, love runs deep.

Time may bend, but we shall stand,
In the embrace of a timeless land.
Through all seasons, our spirits blend,
The journey of two souls, without end.

Whispers of the Heart

In the quiet of the night,
A soft voice calls to me,
Echoing dreams of love,
Whispers set my spirit free.

Tender secrets linger here,
Beneath the silvery moon,
Each word a gentle sigh,
A melody, a sweet tune.

Time stands still, as we connect,
In shadows and in light,
The heart speaks its truth,
Guiding us through the night.

Moments shared, like fleeting stars,
Illuminating our path,
Together, we are whole,
In this dance of love's math.

So let us cherish these threads,
Woven with love so bright,
For in the whispers of the heart,
We find our endless light.

The Journey of Two Souls

Two souls embark on a quest,
Strangers drawn by fate's embrace,
With every step, they learn,
The beauty of time and space.

Through valleys deep and mountains high,
Their laughter fills the air,
Each shared moment a treasure,
A bond beyond compare.

In the silence, they find peace,
In storms, a steady hand,
Navigating life's vast sea,
Together, they will stand.

Stars above guide their path,
Whispering dreams unseen,
Each challenge faced with courage,
A journey, pure and serene.

As seasons change and years unfold,
Their hearts beat in sync,
Together they write their story,
In love, their spirits ink.

When Stars Align

In the vast celestial dome,
Fates entwined in cosmic dance,
When stars ignite the night sky,
A moment caught in chance.

Wishes whispered on the wind,
Hopes carried by the light,
Hearts collide in harmony,
Guided by the stars' sight.

The universe sings a song,
Of love that's meant to be,
With every twinkle overhead,
We shape our destiny.

Magic lingers in the air,
As shadows softly fade,
In the glow of this alignment,
Our hearts no longer weighed.

So let the cosmos conspire,
To weave our dreams so fine,
For in the fabric of the night,
We find our love divine.

A Dance of Shadows

In the dusk's soft embrace,
Shadows play on the wall,
A waltz of light and dark,
Where silence begins to fall.

Figures twirl gracefully,
In a world that feels alive,
Each movement tells a story,
In shadows, dreams derive.

The whispers of the night air,
Carry laughter and sighs,
As twilight wraps around us,
Beneath the starry skies.

With every step we take,
Lost in a reverie,
We dance through fleeting moments,
In perfect symmetry.

So let us sway together,
In this luminous glow,
For in our dance of shadows,
Our love will always flow.

Pilgrimage of Emotions

In shadows deep, our tears will flow,
With every step, we learn to grow.
A winding path, of joy and pain,
Through whispered fears, we break the chain.

The sun will rise, and hearts will mend,
As time drifts on, our wounds will bend.
We wander far, through storm and sun,
A pilgrimage where love's begun.

The mountains high, the valleys low,
In every turn, our spirits glow.
Embrace the ride, let sadness fade,
In unity, our strength displayed.

With open hearts, we'll seek the light,
Through darkest days, we'll hold on tight.
Our journey's rich, with tales untold,
In every step, our dreams unfold.

Through endless skies, our hopes will soar,
A dance of souls, forevermore.
In every heartbeat, truth remains,
Our pilgrimage through love's domains.

Heartfelt Journeys

Upon the road, where hearts do meet,
We share our dreams, our trials sweet.
With every word, a bond we weave,
In heartfelt journeys, we believe.

Through winding turns, our laughter rings,
In whispered wishes, hope takes wings.
With every tear, a story grows,
In every joy, compassion flows.

The stars above, our guiding light,
Illuminate the path, so bright.
In every step, our spirits sing,
In heartfelt journeys, love takes wing.

Amidst the storms, we find our ground,
In silent moments, peace is found.
With open hearts, we take our flight,
In every heart, a spark ignites.

Through storms and calm, we journey far,
Together shining, like a star.
In every heartbeat, truth is found,
In heartfelt journeys, love's profound.

The Floating Garden of Us

In gentle waves, where colors blend,
A floating garden, love will send.
With petals soft, our dreams arise,
In fragrant breaths, beneath the skies.

We sail along, the currents strong,
In whispered winds, we hum our song.
With hands entwined, we drift so free,
In nature's dance, just you and me.

Our laughter blooms like flowers bright,
In golden hues, we chase the light.
With every glance, the world unfolds,
In floating gardens, love's tale told.

The blooms will sway, in unison grand,
As nature sings, we take a stand.
With open hearts, we'll share our trust,
In floating gardens, life's sweet gust.

Through seasons change, our roots hold tight,
In harmony, we share delight.
With every breeze, our spirits rise,
In floating gardens, love never dies.

Finding Our Way Home

Through winding roads, our path unfolds,
In every turn, a tale retold.
With hopeful hearts, we seek the way,
Finding our home, come what may.

The stars align, our dreams ignite,
In the love we share, we find our light.
With every step, a bond we grow,
Through the unknown, together flow.

The memories rise, like echoes near,
In laughter shared, we conquer fear.
With open arms, we'll brave the storm,
Finding our way, in love we're warm.

With every heartbeat, we hold on tight,
In the darkest nights, we find our sight.
Together strong, through thick and thin,
Finding our way, where love begins.

As dawn breaks clear, and shadows fade,
In each embrace, the past we braid.
With courage bold, we'll forge our plot,
Finding our way, we'll never stop.

Finding Home in Your Eyes

In the depths of your gaze, I find my place,
A sanctuary built with love's soft grace.
Whispers of comfort, so tender and true,
In the warmth of your smile, I feel like new.

Through the storms and the shadows, I stand secure,
For in the light of your eyes, I feel so pure.
Every glance a promise, a hope to unfold,
In the story of us, our hearts have told.

Like stars that align in a night so bright,
Each moment with you turns the dark into light.
With every heartbeat, I silently claim,
In finding my home, I found my name.

Across endless miles, your love is my guide,
Through valleys and peaks, you're ever my side.
A journey together, with hands intertwined,
In the realms of your eyes, my heart has aligned.

Forever I seek, in your gaze I reside,
A world full of wonder, where dreams coincide.
Each glance a new chapter, each sigh a sweet rhyme,
In finding my home, you are my lifetime.

Lanterns in the Fog

Amidst the whispers of the night sky,
Lanterns flicker as shadows drift by.
Each glow a beacon in the thick, cool air,
Guiding lost souls through the whispers of care.

The fog wraps around like a lover's embrace,
With each step we take, we dance through space.
In the stillness, the light finds its way,
Illuminating paths where hope dares to stay.

Voices of dreams echo soft in the mist,
Promises linger that time won't resist.
In the twilight of dusk, our fears turn to dust,
For in lanterns aglow, we find our trust.

The night may be dark, but hearts shine like stars,
With lanterns as guides, we'll heal all our scars.
In this gentle embrace of the silvery glow,
Together we'll wander where few dare to go.

So let the fog swirl, let the chill draw near,
With lanterns in hand, there's nothing to fear.
In the embrace of the night, forever we'll log,
Our stories entwined like lanterns in fog.

The Heart's Odyssey

Through uncharted waters, the heart sets sail,
In search of a love that will never grow stale.
With each wave that crashes, a lesson unfolds,
In the journey of life, a treasure to hold.

The stars up above chart the course we must take,
Guiding our ship through the storms we must break.
With every heartbeat, the compass aligns,
In the odyssey of love, our spirit shines.

Through valleys of doubt and mountains of fear,
The heart's true desire is crystal and clear.
For every horizon holds new dreams in store,
And love is the anchor we cherish and adore.

So we'll keep on sailing, through day and through night,
The wind at our backs, our future is bright.
In a world full of wonders, we'll find our way home,
Together forever, in love's sweet poem.

With courage as currency, our dreams will take flight,
In the heart's odyssey, everything feels right.
Every heartbeat a memory, every glance a song,
In the voyage of love, we forever belong.

Stargazing in Twilight

As dusk gently falls and the day bids goodbye,
We lay on the grass, beneath the vast sky.
With comet trails dancing across the hues,
In starlit whispers, our dreams we peruse.

The cool evening air wraps us both tight,
In the stillness of twilight, everything feels right.
Counting the stars as they twinkle and tease,
Each glimmer a story carried on the breeze.

In the tapestry woven with shadows and light,
We find deep connection in the tranquil night.
Every flicker above mirrors sparkles in your eyes,
In stargazing moments, our love never dies.

The universe hums a comforting tune,
As we trace the constellations beneath the moon.
In this cosmic embrace, our spirits take flight,
Together we linger in the magic of night.

With the cosmos as witness, our hearts blend as one,
In the quiet of twilight, our journey's begun.
Each star tells our tale in the skies up above,
In stargazing dreams, we discover our love.

Threads of Destiny

In the loom of fate we weave,
Each thread a story to believe.
Colors blend in patterns bright,
Guiding us through day and night.

Woven dreams that softly gleam,
Reflecting hopes, a shared theme.
With every twist, a chance appears,
To stitch together joy and fears.

Moments linger, gently tied,
In this tapestry, we confide.
Every heartbeat, every laugh,
Forms the fabric of our path.

Through tangled knots and seams that fray,
We find the strength to face the day.
Each thread connects, a bond so true,
Together, we create anew.

In this dance of time and grace,
We find our rhythm, find our place.
Threads of destiny, interlaced,
In life's grand weave, we're embraced.

Embracing Every Step

Every journey starts with one,
A single step towards the sun.
With open arms, I take my flight,
Embracing each new day and night.

Paths may twist and winds may change,
In this dance, I'll not feel strange.
With every step, courage grows,
And who I am, the world now knows.

A leap of faith into the unknown,
Building dreams that feel like home.
With laughter as a guiding star,
I'll chase my goals, no matter how far.

Through trials faced and mountains climbed,
With every heartbeat, I'm reminded.
The beauty lies in the journey made,
In every risk that I have laid.

So here's to moments, big and small,
To every rise, to every fall.
Embracing everything I've met,
I cherish life, I have no regret.

Navigating Through Hearts

In this realm where feelings flow,
Navigating through hearts, we go.
With gentle words and open minds,
Connecting threads that love unwinds.

Every glance, a story shared,
A silent vow, two souls prepared.
To understand, to give, to grow,
In unity, our spirits glow.

Through laughter bright and shadows deep,
We navigate, our bonds to keep.
Guided by trust, we lay our maps,
In every hug, the world perhaps.

With patience, we will chart the seas,
Finding joy in simple pleases.
Hearts entwined, a dance divine,
In this journey, love will shine.

Together as we seek and find,
The treasures that the heart aligned.
Navigating through dreams and art,
Finding solace in each heart.

When Paths Converge

When paths converge, our souls align,
A moment rare, a twist of time.
Like rivers meeting in the night,
Together, we embrace the light.

Two journeys shared, a fusion bright,
Creating warmth in darkest night.
With every step, a spark ignites,
In this union, pure delights.

We find the strength in what we share,
In whispered dreams and tender care.
Together, we will face the storm,
In this embrace, we feel so warm.

As seasons change and moments pass,
We stand as one, in love's sweet glass.
Finding joy in every merge,
With open hearts, our spirits surge.

When paths converge, it's destiny,
A tale of love, you and me.
In every glance, a promise made,
Forever in this dance, we wade.

The Map of Our Dreams

In twilight's glow, we sketch our fate,
With whispered hopes, we navigate.
Stars above, our guiding light,
In the silence, dreams take flight.

Winding paths through fields of gold,
Every story waits to be told.
Together we'll find hidden streams,
Chasing shadows of our dreams.

Mountains rise and rivers flow,
Unforeseen places we long to go.
Adventure calls, we won't delay,
In this map, we find our way.

Through stormy nights and sunny days,
We'll pave our course in varied ways.
Bound by love, we'll journey far,
Each moment shines, like every star.

With every step, new worlds we'll find,
Hearts entwined, two souls aligned.
In this vast expanse, we'll soar,
Hand in hand, forevermore.

A Symphony of Together

In the quiet, our hearts unite,
Creating music, pure delight.
Each note dances in the air,
A symphony beyond compare.

Hands entwined, a gentle clasp,
From this bond, we'll never rasp.
Harmony sings in every glance,
In the rhythm, we find our chance.

Soft whispers weave into the night,
As stars bear witness to our flight.
Melodies rise like morning dew,
In every beat, I feel you too.

Life's a stage where we perform,
Through every storm, love keeps us warm.
In the silence, we hear the sound,
Of love's refrain that knows no bound.

Together, we compose a dream,
A flow of love, a steady beam.
In shared moments, hearts converge,
In this symphony, we will surge.

The Heart's Terrain

In valleys deep, where emotions peak,
We wander through landscapes, unique.
Beneath the skies, so vast and blue,
Our hearts explore, forever true.

Gentle streams that softly flow,
In this terrain, our love will grow.
With every step on this soft ground,
New adventures will be found.

Mountains rise as challenges call,
But united, we shall never fall.
Through rocky paths and winding trails,
Together, love will always prevail.

Seasons change, as time does pass,
In every moment, a dance, a glass.
Embracing life, we brave the storm,
In the heart's terrain, we feel warm.

With every heartbeat, we will chart,
The undying songs of the heart.
Navigating through thick and thin,
Together forever, we shall begin.

The Melody of Us

In quiet corners, our laughter rings,
A melody of sweet, tender things.
With every glance, a song is spun,
In this harmony, we're never done.

Every moment, like notes in the air,
From soft whispers to shouts, we share.
Together, we pen our perfect rhyme,
In the cadence of love, we lose track of time.

With open hearts, we take the lead,
In this rhythm, we plant our seed.
Each heartbeat a cherished refrain,
Echoing softly through joy and pain.

When shadows creep or daylight fades,
In the melody, love never evades.
Through every crescendo, we trust the climb,
Together, we dance, transcending time.

In this symphony, side by side,
Together, in every tide we ride.
Our love's a song that always plays,
In the melody of us, forever stays.

Navigating Love's Labyrinth

In shadows deep, we tread with care,
Hearts entwined, secrets to share.
A twist, a turn, we find our way,
Through love's maze, where dreams will play.

With open minds, we face the night,
Guided by stars, a gentle light.
Each path we walk, both new and old,
A story of love, yet to be told.

In whispers soft, we hear the call,
To stand together, never fall.
With every choice, our souls ignite,
Love's labyrinth shines ever bright.

Through trials vast, we grow so bold,
In passion's fire, our hearts unfold.
Entangled lives, a dance divine,
In love's embrace, forever thine.

As we navigate this winding art,
We cherish moments, heart to heart.
With trust as guide, we journey on,
In love's labyrinth, we're never gone.

The Unfolding of a Story

In quiet corners, tales begin,
Each word a thread, weaves deep within.
From silent pages, whispers rise,
A journey penned, beneath the skies.

With every turn, a lesson found,
Life's precious moments, all around.
Through laughter, tears, the pages turn,
With every chapter, hearts will learn.

In the ink of night, dreams take flight,
Stories echo, banishing fright.
Bound by the tales that gently weave,
In every heart, stories believe.

A tapestry of joy and sorrow,
Each line a promise of tomorrow.
As words come alive, they softly sing,
The unfolding of a life, a precious thing.

Together we'll write, hand in hand,
In this grand story, we understand.
Every ending holds a new start,
In the unfolding, we find our heart.

Wings of Understanding

In delicate flight, the heart can soar,
With wings of love, we seek to explore.
Through trials faced, we learn to bend,
With open hearts, our spirits mend.

In gentle words, we find our way,
Through storms of doubt, love leads the play.
Each layer peeled, a truth revealed,
With wings of understanding, we're healed.

In grace we rise, on currents strong,
Through highs and lows, where we belong.
The skies may darken, but still we fly,
With empathy's wings, we'll touch the sky.

To see each other, as we truly are,
In the light of love, we're never far.
Together in flight, we learn to trust,
With wings of understanding, we must.

As we journey through, side by side,
In every moment, love's our guide.
With open hearts, we rise above,
On wings of understanding, we move with love.

The Echo Chamber of Emotions

In depths of feelings, echoes play,
Whispers of joy, sadness on display.
In chambers vast, emotions swell,
A symphony of tales to tell.

From laughter's light, to shadows deep,
In every heartbeat, secrets keep.
The walls may tremble with every sound,
In the echo chamber, truth is found.

Each emotion calls, a vibrant hue,
Painting our lives in shades so true.
The highs and lows, a dance of grace,
In this echo, we find our place.

As echoes fade, new voices rise,
Through valleys low and endless skies.
In harmony, we share our plight,
In this chamber of emotions, we unite.

Through every clash, we learn to see,
The beauty in our shared decree.
In the echo chamber, we come alive,
With hearts entwined, we learn to thrive.

Reflections in Still Water

Calm surface, whispers below,
Mirror of all that I know.
Time stands still, thoughts collide,
Secrets swim, where dreams abide.

Moonlight dances on cool glass,
Softly guiding shadows past.
Echoes of a distant song,
In this peace, I feel I belong.

Rays of sun in morning glow,
Painting ripples, moving slow.
Nature's voice, a gentle call,
In this serenity, I find it all.

Leaves afloat, secrets shared,
Each reflection, gently bared.
Heart at rest, a soothing balm,
Water's embrace, forever calm.

In stillness, I find my way,
Guided by the light of day.
Through the depths, I softly tread,
In reflections, where dreams are fed.

Navigating the Stars

In the night, my compass glows,
Pathways traced where stardust flows.
Guided by the moon's soft light,
Navigating the endless night.

Constellations whisper tales,
Of ancient battles, lovers' wails.
In their dance, I find my place,
Caught in time's eternal grace.

Shooting stars like wishes fly,
Carried high across the sky.
Holding dreams within my heart,
In this vastness, we're never apart.

Nebulas bloom in colors bright,
Painting stories under the night.
I chart my course through space and time,
In every comet, I see a rhyme.

As the cosmos spins and sways,
Hope ignites in myriad ways.
With each breath, I find I roam,
Navigating the stars, I am home.

Through the Garden of Dreams

In twilight's glow, I wander light,
Through blossoms soft, in quiet night.
Whispers of hope, a gentle breeze,
Awakening my heart with ease.

Petals brush against my skin,
In this realm, I lose, I win.
Colors swirl like thoughts in flight,
Creating peace, a pure delight.

The fragrance of wishes fill the air,
In every shadow, dreams laid bare.
Moonlight filters through the trees,
Stirring my soul, like whispered pleas.

Beneath the stars, my spirit bold,
In secret paths, new tales unfold.
I gather treasures, soft and rare,
In the garden, I find my prayer.

With each step, the magic grows,
In the garden, where the heart knows.
Through dreams I walk, hand in hand,
In this sacred, enchanted land.

The Essence of You

In your smile, the sun breaks through,
A warmth that paints the world anew.
Every laugh, a melody sweet,
In your presence, my heart skips a beat.

Eyes like stars, shining bright,
Holding stories of endless night.
In your gaze, I find my way,
Each moment cherished, come what may.

Your voice, a balm to weary souls,
Every word, a thread that rolls.
Woven dreams in whispered tones,
In your essence, my heart finds homes.

Together we dance through time and space,
Every heartbeat, a warm embrace.
In the silence, our spirits sing,
The essence of you, my everything.

As seasons change, love will stay,
Like sun-kissed skies at the break of day.
In this life, I choose anew,
Every heartbeat echoes you.

Echoes of Affection

Whispers travel soft and low,
Carried on the winds that blow.
Hearts entwined in gentle grace,
In every love, we find our place.

Memories linger, sweet and clear,
Each moment shared, we hold dear.
Through laughter, tears, and silent sighs,
Echoes of affection never die.

Beneath the stars, our dreams ignite,
As shadows dance in the soft moonlight.
Together we weave a tale so bright,
In the canvas of the night.

Time may pass, yet still we stand,
Hand in hand, we understand.
The bond we share grows ever strong,
In the melody of our song.

Through every storm, we find a way,
Guided by love, come what may.
With each echo, our souls align,
In the rhythm of hearts that shine.

Bridges Built with Kindness

Across the chasms wide and deep,
Bridges built, our promises keep.
With every act, a stone is laid,
In kindness, we will never fade.

Hands extended, hearts in flow,
Creating paths where rivers go.
Together we rise, we mend the night,
With beams of hope, we find the light.

Through trials faced and fears embraced,
Our bridges stand, no love misplaced.
Each kindness shared, a step we take,
In unity, we shall awake.

As seasons shift and moments change,
Our hearts, connected, rearrange.
Embracing all in open arms,
In kindness lives the greatest charms.

When storms may rage, and clouds may hide,
We'll stand as one, side by side.
In every heartbeat, bonds will grow,
Love's bridge remains, steadfast and slow.

The Compass of Togetherness

In every journey we embark,
A compass guides us through the dark.
With every turn, we learn to see,
The beauty in our harmony.

Through winding paths, hand in hand,
Together we rise, together we stand.
With every challenge, we will find,
The strength of love, hearts entwined.

The map is drawn in laughter's hue,
With every laugh, the skies turn blue.
In every tear, a lesson learned,
In the fires of trials, our hearts have burned.

The stars align, a guiding light,
In the depths of the darkest night.
With trust as our unyielding base,
In togetherness, we find our place.

As we navigate this life so vast,
With every moment, memories cast.
The compass spins yet holds us true,
In every journey, I choose you.

Under the Same Star

In a world so vast and wide,
We find our dreams where hopes reside.
Under the same star, we gaze above,
Knitted together, heart by heart, love.

Through whispers shared and secrets kept,
We weave a bond where promises are met.
In the quiet night, our spirits soar,
Under the same star, we yearn for more.

With each dawn that brings the light,
We chase our dreams, ready to fight.
Though paths may twist and sometimes part,
Under the same star, we share one heart.

In every sunset, painted gold,
Stories of love and courage unfold.
Through trials faced with open minds,
Under the same star, our love binds.

As shadows fade and stars ignite,
We'll dance in the moon's soft, silver light.
Together we'll stand, never apart,
Under the same star, forever in heart.

The Radiance of Unity

In the glow of dawn's first light,
We gather hearts, a bond so tight.
Together, we weave dreams anew,
In every laugh, in every hue.

Through trials faced, we stand as one,
A tapestry from threads we've spun.
In unity, our spirits soar,
A symphony that we explore.

Hand in hand, we walk this shore,
Each step, a song we can restore.
In shadows deep and moments bright,
We shine together, pure delight.

The challenges may come our way,
Yet side by side, we boldly sway.
With open minds, we lift our voice,
In every silence, there's a choice.

In the end, what binds us tight,
Is the radiance of our shared light.
With love as guide, forever true,
Together, we'll see each dream through.

The Alchemy of Affection

In tender whispers, love ignites,
Transforming souls in soft moonlight.
With every touch, a spark we trace,
In shared embrace, we find our place.

Through moments sweet, the laughter flows,
Like rivers deep, affection grows.
In every glance, a magic spell,
A silent prayer, our hearts rebel.

With patience strong, we shape our fate,
In each heartbeat, we resonate.
Alchemy entwined in every kiss,
Upon our lips, a world of bliss.

Through storms we weather, hand in hand,
With love as strong as shifting sand.
In golden hours, we craft our day,
In the alchemy, we find our way.

As seasons change, our roots dig deep,
In bonds of love, our spirits leap.
Together forged, we rise and shine,
In the tapestry of hearts, divine.

The Odyssey of Together

To distant shores, we sail as one,
Beneath the stars, a journey begun.
With every wave, our courage flows,
In shared horizons, love truly grows.

Through uncharted lands, we wander free,
With hearts aligned, just you and me.
In the laughter, in the tears we share,
Together facing all, we bravely dare.

With every tale, our bond expands,
In mystery's embrace, we make our plans.
Through trials fierce, we claim our prize,
In every sunset, hope arises.

In radiant dawns, we find our way,
With every heartbeat, we convey.
A voyage shared, forever cast,
In memories made, our shadows last.

So let us chart this course anew,
With love as compass, tried and true.
In this odyssey, as paths converge,
Together, we feel the world emerge.

The Harmony of Two Voices

In the quiet, where whispers meet,
Two voices rise, a melody sweet.
In every note, a story told,
In harmony, a bond unfolds.

Through simple words, the heart takes flight,
With every laugh, we find our light.
In symphonies of shared delight,
Together, we dance through day and night.

With every chord, our souls align,
In perfect rhythm, your heart with mine.
The echoes linger, soft and clear,
In this harmony, we conquer fear.

As seasons shift, our song remains,
In joy and sorrow, love sustains.
With every breath, a promise made,
In two voices, our fears allayed.

So let us sing till stars grow dim,
In every lyric, we find the hymn.
In this duet, forever soar,
The harmony of us, evermore.

The Lanterns of Devotion

In the quiet night we stand,
Holding lanterns in our hands.
Their glow a symbol, warm and bright,
Guiding our hearts through the night.

Together we share this sacred light,
Shadows dance in the tender sight.
Through storms and trials, we will shine,
With every flicker, your hand in mine.

Oh, how the breeze whispers our names,
In this beauty, nothing feels the same.
With faith as our anchor, the world we face,
In devotion's embrace, we find our place.

Each lantern drifts, a story told,
A flame of love, we hold so bold.
Through the trials, our spirits soar,
In this devotion, forevermore.

Beyond the Horizon of Us

Glimmers of dawn paint the sky,
With every heartbeat, time slips by.
Together we chase the fading light,
Dreams unfurling, taking flight.

Across the waves, our laughter rings,
In the distance, the seagull sings.
Hand in hand, we wander far,
Chasing sunsets, our guiding star.

Through valleys deep and mountains high,
With whispered hopes, we learn to fly.
The horizon beckons, wide and vast,
A promise of futures, forever cast.

In every step, a rhythm flows,
Our souls entwined as the river glows.
For beyond the horizon, love will steer,
In the tapestry of life, you are near.

Stitched with Tenderness

In the quiet of the evening's grace,
We find warmth in each other's space.
Every stitch, a memory sewn,
In fabric, love is gently grown.

With every thread, a story told,
Soft and warm, against the cold.
Tender moments, woven tight,
Each embrace feels just right.

Through trials faced and joys embraced,
In every tear, our love replaced.
With strength like threads that hold us near,
Stitched with tenderness, I fear no fear.

Every pattern, uniquely ours,
A tapestry beneath the stars.
In this quilt of life, we blend,
Two souls that dance, and never end.

Footprints on Shared Soil

In the garden where we sow,
Footprints left in gentle flow.
Each step a mark, a love defined,
Together, our lives intertwined.

Through fields of green, we wander free,
Each little moment feels like glee.
With laughter carried on the breeze,
In shared soil, we find our ease.

As seasons change, new paths appear,
Yet hand in hand, we conquer fear.
Through rivers wide and mountains steep,
In shared soil, our promises keep.

A journey blessed, our hearts in tune,
In every dawn, a bright new moon.
With every footprint, a story grows,
In shared soil, true love bestows.

Uncharted Embrace

In a world where shadows play,
We wander far, come what may.
With whispers soft like morning dew,
We find a bond, both brave and true.

Through tangled paths, we chart our course,
With hope as our guiding force.
In every glance, a story told,
An uncharted embrace, brave and bold.

The stars align in twilight's grace,
Two souls entwined in time and space.
With every heartbeat, we explore,
In this unknown, we crave for more.

Together we will rise and roam,
In distant lands, we'll call it home.
Hand in hand, we meet the night,
In uncharted dreams, we find our light.

As dawn breaks forth with golden sheen,
Our journey blooms, a vibrant scene.
In every trail, love's footprints trace,
An everlasting, uncharted embrace.

Hearts in Harmony

Two hearts, a melody so sweet,
In rhythm dance, they find their beat.
With every note, our spirits soar,
In harmony, we want for more.

The world outside fades to gray,
But in our song, we choose to stay.
Each laugh, each sigh, a gentle rhyme,
In perfect sync, we conquer time.

Through storms and trials, we will sing,
With every chord, new hopes take wing.
Together strong, we face the tide,
In hearts united, we will bide.

With whispers sweet, the night reveals,
Our dreams entwined, the truth it feels.
In every heartbeat, passion flows,
In hearts' embrace, our love just grows.

Side by side, we'll paint the skies,
In sunsets bright, our spirits rise.
A symphony that time won't part,
We dance forever, hearts in heart.

Footprints in the Sand

Upon the shore where waves retreat,
We leave our marks, both soft and sweet.
Each step we take, a tale unfolds,
In whispered winds, our journey holds.

With tides that ebb and flow with grace,
We find our path in this warm space.
Footprints linger where dreams expand,
In golden light, we take our stand.

As sunset bleeds into the night,
We trace our steps in fading light.
In every grain, the stories blend,
Footprints left for time to mend.

With every wave, a memory kissed,
In fleeting time, we can't desist.
Through storms that come, we will remain,
With love as strong as any chain.

Together we will face the tide,
With hearts as one, we will confide.
In every footprint in the sand,
A love that's true, forever planned.

The Orchard of Secrets

In hidden groves where whispers bloom,
The orchard thrives, dispelling gloom.
With every fruit, a secret shared,
In twilight's glow, our hearts laid bare.

Beneath the boughs, we find our peace,
In gentle leaves, our worries cease.
Each shared glance, a moment rare,
In the orchard's heart, love's tender care.

As seasons change, our roots grow deep,
In laughter's shade, we yearn and leap.
The sun will rise, the moon will wane,
In this orchard's embrace, none remain.

With every harvest, stories soar,
In fragrant air, we seek for more.
In every branch, a tale to tell,
Among these trees, we fell under spell.

A treasure trove, where dreams collide,
In the orchard's heart, we will abide.
With secrets kept and trust so grand,
Together here, we take our stand.

Blossoms of Devotion

In the garden where we tread,
Petals whisper secrets said.
With each bloom, love intertwines,
Silent vows in fragrant lines.

Sunlight dances on our skin,
A gentle breeze, where dreams begin.
In every shade, a hope we find,
Nature's touch, forever kind.

Through seasons change, we stay so near,
Blooming hearts, we persevere.
With roots so deep, we grow as one,
A symphony, we've just begun.

Under stars, our wishes soar,
In moonlit night, we long for more.
Together, hand in hand we stand,
In love's embrace, a promise grand.

Each flower tells a tale so true,
In every hue, my heart's with you.
From bud to blossom, we will thrive,
In devotion, we come alive.

The Rhythm of Us

In the silence, our hearts beat,
A melody both soft and sweet.
Each glance shared, a note on high,
Together, we will touch the sky.

Through the chaos, we compose,
Harmony that gently grows.
With every laugh, a dance we weave,
A rhythm forged, we dare believe.

As seasons change, so do our songs,
In love's embrace, we both belong.
With every step, we create anew,
The cadence of me, the pulse of you.

Our laughter rings like chimes in air,
A symphony beyond compare.
In whispers soft, our hearts will trust,
In perfect time, the rhythm of us.

With every beat, together we flow,
In every high, in every low.
A journey where our spirits dance,
In the rhythm of love's sweet trance.

Harmonizing Destinies

Two paths converged, fate drew near,
In the twilight, dreams appear.
Every choice a chord we play,
Together, we'll find our way.

With open hearts, we dare to glide,
In this journey, side by side.
With each moment, a note so clear,
In harmony, we grasp the year.

Sweet serendipity, our light,
Guiding stars throughout the night.
In every struggle, we will rise,
With trust as deep as endless skies.

When storms arise and shadows fall,
Our melody, it lifts us all.
Each twist and turn, a chance to mend,
Together, my love, we transcend.

With dreams united, we'll explore,
In every heartbeat, we'll restore.
In life's great song, we'll find our peace,
Harmonizing, our souls release.

A Compass of Kindness

In a world that spins so fast,
With gentle hearts, our love will last.
With open hands, we pave the way,
A compass of kindness leads each day.

In every smile, a spark ignites,
Through simple acts, we share our lights.
In quiet moments, we choose to care,
With warmth and grace, our hearts lay bare.

Through trials faced and burdens shared,
A guiding star, we are prepared.
Together we can mend the seams,
With kindness sewn in every dream.

With words so soft, we lift each other,
In unity, we find our brother.
In laughter shared, our spirits soar,
With every kindness, we explore.

In this journey, let love lead,
In every act, plant a seed.
For in our souls, the truth we find,
A compass of kindness, truly kind.

Threads of Connection

In the quiet hum of night,
Whispers weave through the air,
Hearts stitched with gentle light,
Binding souls with tender care.

From the laughter, bonds emerge,
Like vines entwining in grace,
In every hug, a gentle surge,
Distance fades in love's embrace.

The stories shared, a tapestry,
Woven with dreams and fears,
Each thread a part of history,
Strengthened through the years.

Through storms that life will send,
The fibers hold us tight,
Connection that will not bend,
A beacon in the night.

So let us cherish and uphold,
The ties that keep us near,
In every thread, a story told,
Love's fabric, ever dear.

Celestial Compass

The stars align in midnight's hush,
Guiding hearts with ancient light,
In a cosmic dance, a gentle rush,
Navigating dreams in the night.

Planets twirl in graceful arcs,
Whispers of fate in the sky,
Each spark a sign, igniting sparks,
As we wander and ask the why.

Comets streak with fleeting grace,
Marking paths we dare to trace,
With every heartbeat, we find our place,
In the universe's vast embrace.

Galaxies spin in silent motion,
Mapping journeys yet untold,
Through the cosmos, a boundless ocean,
Where destinies unfold.

Follow the light that beckons near,
A compass of dreams to steer,
In the night, let go of fear,
Embrace the journey, crystal clear.

Navigating the Unknown

A path obscured by mist and doubt,
Footsteps falter, hearts unsure,
Yet in the whispers, there's a shout,
A promise found within the pure.

With every step into the haze,
Curiosity blooms like a flower,
In darkness, we learn to gaze,
Discovering strength, a hidden power.

The compass of hope points the way,
Casting light on shadowed fears,
Through winding roads, we dance and sway,
Embracing change through all the years.

We breathe in courage, exhale despair,
With every challenge, we ignite,
The world unfolds, rich and rare,
A tapestry stitched in the night.

So take my hand, let's weave through fate,
In the unknown, we will grow,
Together we'll learn, together create,
In the journey, let love flow.

The Unraveled Thread

In the quiet of a fading day,
A thread unravels, soft and slow,
Tales of yesterdays slip away,
Leaving behind a gentle glow.

Memories dance like leaves in fall,
Spinning whims of joy and pain,
Each moment whispers, hear the call,
In the unraveling, there's a gain.

The fabric of life, thin and worn,
Frayed edges tell of battles fought,
From the chaos, beauty is born,
In the mess, our lessons taught.

With every twist, a story fades,
Yet hope remains in threads anew,
In the silence, where courage pervades,
We stitch our dreams, create our view.

Embrace the threads that once were tight,
And weave them with love once more,
For in the unraveling, find the light,
A tapestry worth fighting for.

Riding the Waves of Connection

In the swell of the ocean's might,
We find our hearts in gentle flight.
Waves crash softly, whispers play,
Binding our souls in a dance today.

Tides of laughter, currents strong,
Together we sing our vibrant song.
Each ripple tells a story shared,
In this embrace, we are both bared.

The horizon beckons, stars align,
In the depths, our spirits entwine.
Each wave a heartbeat, pure and true,
In this vast sea, it's me and you.

Surfing dreams on morning's light,
With every rise, we gain new height.
Connection deepens as we glide,
With love as our steady guide.

Through storms we weather, hand in hand,
On this adventure, we take a stand.
In our journey, we find the way,
Together forever, come what may.

A Journey Imprinted in Time

Footprints etched in sand and stone,
Every step taken, never alone.
The path unwinds beneath our feet,
Memories linger, so bittersweet.

Each turning point, a lesson learned,
In the flames of passion, we have burned.
Time unfolds like petals in bloom,
Coloring life in light and gloom.

With every sunset, shadows creep,
In dreams and whispers, secrets keep.
We travel roads both near and far,
Guided by the light of our star.

In the tapestry, threads intertwine,
Patterns of fate, a grand design.
Through laughter and tears, we have grown,
In the chronicles of love, we have flown.

As seasons change, we remain true,
In the dance of life, it's me and you.
Imprints of joy, pains left behind,
In the heart's journey, forever entwined.

The Canvas of Our Intentions

Brush strokes of hope, colors collide,
In the canvas of life, side by side.
Each hue a story, each line a dream,
In the gallery of our hearts, we beam.

With every painting, our visions align,
Crafting a world that feels divine.
Splashes of laughter, whispers of light,
Creating a masterpiece, ever so bright.

Layers of trust in vibrant blend,
With each stroke, we learn, we mend.
Shadows may linger, but that's the art,
Finding the beauty before we part.

Sketches of memories forever hold,
The tales of our journey, bright and bold.
With every creation, we find our peace,
In the gallery of time, may love never cease.

Together we boldly create our fate,
In the palette of life, we celebrate.
The canvas speaks of the bonds we share,
In this vivid world, a love laid bare.

Finding Solace in Each Other

In the quiet of the night, we rest,
Finding comfort in each other's zest.
Whispers of dreams drift through the air,
In these moments, we lay our souls bare.

Against the storm, we stand so strong,
In your embrace, I feel I belong.
Each heartbeat echoes a tender vow,
Together we rise, here and now.

Gentle laughter in the softest glow,
In your eyes, I find a warmth that flows.
When the world is loud, and doubts arise,
In your presence, the chaos dies.

With every tear, we learn to heal,
In shared silence, our truths reveal.
Finding solace, just you and I,
In this sacred space, we can't deny.

Through every challenge, we will endure,
In this love, we find the cure.
As we breathe in this sweet refrain,
Finding solace in each other's pain.

Beneath the Same Sky

We gaze at stars that weave,
A tapestry of dreams we share.
Under the moonlight's gentle glow,
A silent bond that few can dare.

In whispers carried by the breeze,
Our hopes collide like waves on shore.
Together we discover peace,
Beneath the sky, we long for more.

With every sunset's vibrant hue,
We paint our stories, side by side.
Each moment captured, ever true,
In this vast world, we dare to guide.

The clouds may drift, the night may fall,
Yet love, it binds us, thread by thread.
In harmony, we answer the call,
Beneath the same sky, forever led.

So let's embrace this endless flight,
With hearts entwined, we'll journey far.
Side by side, we'll chase the light,
Together, beneath the same star.

The Quest for Belonging

In a world where voices stray,
We search for hearts that truly see.
Through valleys deep and mountains high,
The quest for home, our shared decree.

With every step, we seek to find,
A place where shadows lose their bite.
Among the echoes of our hearts,
We yearn for warmth, for love, for light.

Through laughter shared and sorrow's tears,
Connections bloom, a fragile thread.
In every smile, we banish fears,
In unity, our spirits spread.

As wanderers, we roam the night,
Yet long for shelter, arms embraced.
In bonds of trust, we'll find our right,
A sanctuary, our hearts interlaced.

So let us gather, hand in hand,
In this vast life, let love belong.
Through every challenge, we will stand,
Our journey's hymn, a timeless song.

Serendipitous Encounters

Amidst the crowd, a fleeting glance,
Two souls collide, the spark ignites.
In moments brief, we take a chance,
The universe concedes its rights.

From stranger's smile to laughter shared,
We dance in fate's uncharted game.
In serendipity, we're bared,
As life unfolds, we'll never be the same.

Each twist of fate, an open door,
A chance encounter, hearts align.
In whispers soft, we crave for more,
These moments precious, pure, divine.

With every step we forge a path,
Where destinies entwine as one.
Through joy and warmth, we leave our path,
In serendipitous love, we're spun.

So cherish these fleeting gatherings,
The magic woven in each smile.
For every meet, a gift it brings,
A tapestry of dreams worthwhile.

A Symphony of Hearts

In every heartbeat, songs arise,
A melody of souls entwined.
We hear the rhythm of the skies,
In love's embrace, our fates aligned.

Each note a whisper, sweet and clear,
A symphony that binds us tight.
Through laughter, sorrow, hope, and fear,
Together we compose the night.

The chords of life, they ebb and flow,
Like waves that crash upon the shore.
In harmony, our spirits grow,
Within this music, we explore.

With every breath, we take our part,
An anthem built on trust and care.
In unity, we sing from heart,
A symphony that we all share.

So let us raise our voices high,
In celebration of our days.
For in this life, beneath the sky,
We find our strength in love's sweet ways.

The Architecture of Us

In the quiet halls of dreams,
Designs of heartbeats play,
Brick by brick, we build our home,
In the light of each new day.

Walls echo with laughter's sound,
Windows that frame our grace,
Roofs sheltering whispered vows,
A sacred, warm embrace.

Foundations forged in trust so deep,
Blueprints sketched in time,
Each moment adds a floor,
To this structure so sublime.

Rooms filled with tender touch,
Stairways leading high,
In the architecture of us,
Love will never die.

Together we shall rise,
In this fortress strong and true,
With every stone we place,
I choose to be with you.

Journeys of the Heart

Paths we walk, hand in hand,
Through valleys low, peaks so grand,
Each step a promise, softly spoken,
In every silence, bonds unbroken.

Winding roads, the sun will set,
We chase horizons, no regret,
In every turn, a new surprise,
Love's adventure never dies.

Seasons change, we feel the pull,
Like tides that rise, our hearts are full,
Navigating through the storm,
In our embrace, we find the warm.

Stories written in the skies,
With every glance, we realize,
Together through the joy and pain,
In the dance of love, we will remain.

Journeys weave a tapestry,
Of dreams and hopes we long to see,
In every heartbeat, every sigh,
We journey forth, you and I.

The Essence of Together

In the silence of the night,
Your heartbeat is my light,
In the chaos of the day,
You're the calm that guides my way.

Every glance, a story told,
In your smile, I find my gold,
Moments shared, like stars align,
In your essence, I see mine.

Whispers shared beneath the moon,
In your presence, I feel in tune,
Every breath, a shared delight,
Together we'll chase the light.

Threads of fate that intertwine,
In the fabric of the divine,
Love's embrace, a sacred tether,
In this life, we are together.

Each heartbeat marks the time we grow,
Through the ebb and flow, we know,
In our journey, hand in hand,
The essence of together stands.

Heartstrings in Symphony

Like notes that dance on gentle breeze,
Our hearts compose a tender ease,
In harmony we find our way,
In every glance, in every sway.

Chords of laughter, sweet and bright,
Melodies under starlit night,
In unison, we sing our song,
Together, where we both belong.

Fingers touch as if to play,
The symphony of love each day,
With every beat, our spirits soar,
In this music, evermore.

Echoes of the dreams we share,
In this rhythm, we're laid bare,
Love's crescendo, rising high,
In our symphony, we fly.

Together through the night and day,
In perfect time, we find our way,
Heartstrings intertwined as one,
In our music, we have won.

Lanterns Along the Way

In the quiet night, they glow,
Guiding hearts with warmth below.
Every flicker tells a tale,
Of journeys taken, love's sweet trail.

Beneath the stars, they softly sway,
Casting shadows where we play.
Each lantern holds a whispered wish,
In the dark, a glowing fish.

Together we walk, hand in hand,
Finding comfort in this land.
With each step, a bond we weave,
In lantern light, we dare believe.

The night unfolds, our feelings grow,
As lanterns dance, our spirits flow.
In this moment, time does freeze,
Love illuminates, brings us ease.

With every lantern, a promise made,
Hope shines bright, never to fade.
We follow paths both old and new,
In the light, we find what's true.

The Realm of Shared Dreams

In twilight's glow, our dreams unite,
We wander free, hearts taking flight.
In whispered hopes, we venture deep,
To worlds where love is ours to keep.

Together we sketch the stars above,
A canvas painted with our love.
Each dream a thread in fabric spun,
Ties that bind us, two as one.

In every laugh, in every sigh,
We reach for skies, our spirits high.
The realm of dreams, where we both soar,
A place of peace, forevermore.

With every heartbeat, visions gleam,
In the quiet dark, we dare to dream.
A journey bright, hand in hand we roam,
In this vast space, we find our home.

As dawn breaks forth, our dreams still stay,
Guiding us through each new day.
In the realm of shared embrace,
We find our truth, our sacred space.

Planted in Each Other's Hearts

In gardens rich with love, we grow,
Roots entwined beneath the snow.
Each tender shoot breaks through the ground,
In every glance, affection found.

With gentle hands, we tend the soil,
Nurturing dreams with endless toil.
Sunshine warms, and rain bestows,
A bond that deepens as it flows.

Through all seasons, we stand as one,
Facing storms until they're done.
In winter's chill, our warmth ignites,
Together we bloom, reaching heights.

With open hearts, we share our fears,
Watered with laughter, joy, and tears.
Planted firmly, our roots can't part,
Love's garden thrives within each heart.

The blossoms dance in gentle breeze,
A melody of love that frees.
In every petal, a story starts,
Planted deep in each other's hearts.

The Pulse of Togetherness

In the rhythm of our shared embrace,
We find a steady, sacred space.
With every heartbeat, we align,
A pulse that sings, forever fine.

In laughter's echo, joy resounds,
A symphony of love surrounds.
Through trials faced, our bond grows strong,
In every note, where we belong.

With gentle words and quiet sighs,
We weave our lives beneath the skies.
The pulse of togetherness we share,
A dance of souls, a love laid bare.

In moonlit nights, we stand as one,
As time slips by, our hearts have won.
In every moment, we find reprieve,
Together, in this love, we believe.

In the stillness, hearts entwined,
The pulse of peace, so well defined.
Through every storm, we'll find our way,
In love's embrace, we choose to stay.

Vows Written in the Stars

Underneath the endless sky,
We whispered promises so high.
With constellations as our guide,
In this love, we both confide.

Fate has woven threads so bright,
Twinkling softly in the night.
Every star a cherished dream,
In the dark, our hearts do gleam.

Together we will always stand,
With the universe at hand.
In the twilight, hearts align,
Forever bound, your hand in mine.

Though storms may try to tear us apart,
We'll navigate with steadfast heart.
Each vow is written in the skies,
In every glance, our love complies.

As the cosmos holds our names,
In its vastness, love inflames.
Through galaxies, we'll roam free,
With the stars as company.

Roots Intertwined

In the soil where we began,
Two souls meet, like a plan.
Deep below, where shadows dwell,
Our roots entwine, under a spell.

With every season, we do grow,
Through the sun and through the snow.
In this garden, love takes flight,
Nourished by the stars at night.

Through the years, we'll stand so strong,
Together where we both belong.
Branches reaching for the sky,
In this embrace, we'll never die.

When storms do come, our bonds will bend,
But never will our love descend.
Intertwined, we'll weather all,
With every rise, together we fall.

So let the roots speak our tales,
Of love that dances, never fails.
Through life's seasons, hand in hand,
Roots intertwined, we'll ever stand.

Sailing into Tomorrow

Set our sails to the bright unknown,
Waves of hope that we have sown.
Guided by the sun's warm light,
We embark into the night.

With every breeze, we chase our dreams,
Navigating life's glowing streams.
Together, we won't drift apart,
With every tide, we sail with heart.

Horizons wide, the world our own,
In search of treasures yet unshown.
Fate will chart our course so true,
In every wave, I'll find you.

Though storms may rage and skies turn gray,
In your eyes, I find my way.
With laughter, we'll harness the swell,
On this journey, all is well.

Hand in hand, we face the dawn,
With every moment, we grow strong.
Sailing into tomorrow's light,
Together, forever in flight.

A Path Lit by Kindness

On gentle trails where we have walked,
Kindness blooms in every talk.
With every step, compassion grows,
In our hearts, a warm light glows.

Through the thicket, we will share,
Love and hope fill the air.
Every smile is a guiding star,
Leading us, no matter how far.

When shadows loom and doubts arise,
Together, we will harmonize.
With open hearts, we break the gloom,
In every act, kindness will bloom.

Through the valleys, we will roam,
In each other, we've found home.
Every gesture, a bridge we build,
With love and kindness, hearts fulfilled.

So let's tread this path with grace,
Bringing light to every place.
In this journey, hand in hand,
A path lit by kindness will stand.

A Quest for Connectedness

In the quiet corners of the night,
We search for echoes of our plight,
Voices whisper, souls entwined,
A journey forged, the ties we bind.

Under starlit skies, we roam,
Mapping paths that lead us home,
Shared laughter on the breeze,
In unity, we find our ease.

In shadows deep, we chase the light,
Embracing warmth, igniting bright,
With every heartbeat, every glance,
Together in this sacred dance.

Through valleys low and mountains high,
We rise above, we touch the sky,
In every tear, in every grin,
The quest for love begins within.

And as we tread this sacred land,
With open hearts and outstretched hands,
Connected souls, we stand as one,
In this vast world, our journey's begun.

Tracing Lines of Affection

With gentle strokes, we draw our fate,
Lines of love we carefully create,
Each moment shared, a mark we find,
In the tapestry of hearts combined.

From whispered words to tender touch,
These threads of care mean so much,
In every laugh, in every sigh,
A masterpiece worth every try.

Through seasons change, our colors blend,
In woven bonds that never bend,
Tracing paths of memories past,
In the art of love, we hold steadfast.

In every heartbeat, lines we trace,
A canvas rich in warm embrace,
Through storms and calm, we'll stand our ground,
In every corner, affection found.

As stars align through darkened skies,
We sketch our dreams, let spirits rise,
In every moment, love's design,
Forever etched, your heart with mine.

A Sojourn of the Spirit

Wandering through the realms of thought,
In search of solace that can't be bought,
Each step we take, a story grows,
The spirit's journey, nobody knows.

In quiet whispers, secrets hide,
The depths of self where truths abide,
Through trials faced and lessons learned,
The heart ignites, the spirit yearned.

Above the clouds, our dreams take flight,
In shadows cast, we seek the light,
With every challenge, we find our way,
In the sojourn, we learn to play.

In the stillness, reflection calls,
Each rise and fall, each stumble, crawls,
Through the ages, wisdom flows,
The sojourn lasts, as the spirit grows.

And when we sail on life's vast sea,
The shores of peace will set us free,
With open hearts, we journey hence,
The soul's sojourn, our recompense.

Threads of Fate Weaving Together

In the loom of life, we twist and turn,
Threads of fate, for which we yearn,
Every choice a stitch we make,
In this fabric, no hearts break.

Bound by time, our stories blend,
Each moment shared, a message penned,
Through laughter bright and shadows cast,
We weave the future from the past.

In vibrant hues, our dreams unite,
With every pulse, we spark the light,
As fate entwines, we come to know,
The beauty in our shared tableau.

Through trials faced, our strength defines,
The threads of love that intertwines,
In every knot, a tale we find,
In woven hearts, we're all aligned.

And as the tapestry unfolds wide,
With open hearts, we stand beside,
In destiny's embrace, we'll stay,
Threads of fate, forever sway.

Echoes of Affection

Whispers linger in the night,
Softly calling, hearts in flight.
Memories dance like gentle streams,
Filling silence with sweet dreams.

Laughter captured in the air,
Moments cherished, love laid bare.
In every glance, a story spun,
Echoes of two hearts as one.

Time may fade, yet feelings stay,
In the twilight's soft array.
Holding close what words can't say,
Echoes of affection sway.

Through the shadows, light will shine,
Binding souls, your hand in mine.
Every heartbeat, every sigh,
Lives forever, you and I.

So let us dance this tender waltz,
In the rhythm, find no faults.
With every step, a promise made,
Echoes of affection won't fade.

Beneath the Banyan Tree

Beneath the branches, shadows play,
Whispers of love in the light of day.
Roots embrace the earth so tight,
Holding secrets of pure delight.

Leaves rustle softly in the breeze,
Carrying tales of memories seized.
In this haven, time stands still,
Needing nothing, just your will.

Sunlight dapples on the ground,
In the stillness, peace is found.
Our laughter echoes, pure and true,
Beneath the banyan, just me and you.

Even storms may weave their way,
Yet our bond will never sway.
Together strong, we face the fight,
Beneath the banyan, all feels right.

As seasons change and shadows grow,
Love like ours will always flow.
In nature's arms, we're intertwined,
Beneath the banyan, hearts aligned.

The Map of Us

On this canvas, strokes of fate,
Drawn together, love can't wait.
Paths entwined, our journeys merge,
In every heartbeat, passions surge.

With every step, we write a tale,
A map of dreams where love won't fail.
Markers placed in joy and tears,
Mapping moments through the years.

Through mountains high and valleys low,
Hand in hand, together we go.
Compass set on love's embrace,
Guiding us through time and space.

In the ink of stars above,
Every line speaks of our love.
Navigating wild and free,
The map of us is destiny.

Adventure calls, the world awaits,
With open hearts, we watch the gates.
We'll chart our course, no road is lost,
The map of us is worth the cost.

Tides of Tenderness

Waves crash softly on the shore,
Each caress whispers, 'I adore.'
The moonlight dances on the sea,
In every tide, my heart speaks free.

Moments ripple, ebb and flow,
In this love, we come to know.
With each wave, a gentle kiss,
Tides of tenderness bring bliss.

Stories written in the sand,
Nature's blessings, hand in hand.
Every sunset paints our sky,
As the tides draw nigh, we sigh.

Through storms that test our will,
Love's anchor holds, it won't be still.
In the quiet, we'll find peace,
Tides of tenderness, love's release.

So let the currents guide our ways,
In this sea, love's light displays.
Together always, side by side,
Tides of tenderness, our guide.

Dreams in the Garden of Us

In twilight's gentle whispering light,
We plant our hopes, take flight.
Petals of laughter softly sway,
In this garden, dreams come to play.

With every drop of dew that falls,
We listen close to nature's calls.
The fragrance of love fills the air,
A sacred space, our hearts laid bare.

Sunshine beams on moments we share,
In this haven, nothing can compare.
Growing together, hand in hand,
In the soil of dreams, we make our stand.

Whispers of secrets linger here,
In the shadows, we face our fear.
Roots entwined, we find our way,
In this garden, we forever stay.

Even when storms threaten our peace,
Our trust in love will never cease.
Through every season, we remain,
In the garden, we find the gain.

A Voyage of Trust

Sailing on waves of deep emotion,
Guided by hearts, a potent potion.
In the vast expanse, we find our way,
Through storms and calm, come what may.

Anchored in faith, we set our course,
Drawing strength from love's true source.
Every heartbeat, a rhythmic tide,
In this journey, we're side by side.

Stars above, a map of dreams,
Navigating life, or so it seems.
Each new horizon, a tale to tell,
In the ocean of trust, we dwell.

Even as shadows loom so near,
We embrace the waves, conquer our fear.
Together we weather the fiercest blasts,
In the vessel of love, we're unsurpassed.

With every sunrise, we start anew,
Charting courses, me and you.
In this voyage, our spirits intertwined,
A tapestry of trust, beautifully designed.

Melodies of Connection

In the silence, a gentle strum,
Notes of love, they softly come.
Harmony found in every glance,
Together we weave our sweet romance.

With every chord, a story told,
In the warmth of smiles, we behold.
Each laugh a rhythm, pure and bright,
Our souls dance together, taking flight.

Fingers tracing along the lines,
In this moment, our heart aligns.
The melody lingers, sweet and clear,
In this symphony, love draws near.

As the world fades to a hush,
Our hearts thrumming in a rush.
Each beat a promise, strong and sure,
In this connection, we find our cure.

Through ups and downs, we sing our song,
A duet of life, where we belong.
In the echoes of laughter and tears,
The melody of love transcends the years.

Beneath the Canopy of Us

Under the shelter of leafy dreams,
Where sunlight filters and softly gleams.
Fingers entwined, we find our peace,
In this haven, worries cease.

The rustling leaves whisper our names,
Under their watch, love boldly flames.
Each moment spent beneath this dome,
In nature's arms, we find our home.

As shadows dance in the fading light,
We cherish each heartbeat, holding tight.
The branches sway with secrets untold,
In this sanctuary, love unfolds.

Our laughter mingles with the breeze,
An orchestra playing through the trees.
In the embrace of the great expanse,
We pledge our love with every glance.

With each season, leaves will turn,
In this canopy, still we yearn.
Forever grounded, come what may,
Beneath the canopy, we shall stay.

Uncharted Territories of the Heart

In silent whispers, secrets dwell,
Unknown paths where feelings swell.
With every breath, a new embrace,
In the twilight, we find our place.

Stars above, they guide our way,
Through shadows deep, we choose to stay.
With open hearts, we brave the night,
Exploring dreams, chasing the light.

The tides of time, they ebb and flow,
In unison, our spirits grow.
A dance of souls, entwined as one,
Together we shine, like the sun.

Maps uncharted, drawn in air,
Every glance, a silent prayer.
Vows unspoken, hearts in flight,
In the darkness, you are my light.

Together we roam, wild and free,
With every heartbeat, harmony.
In the labyrinth of what we feel,
The uncharted lands become our real.

Harmonious Frequencies

In waves of sound, we rise and fall,
A symphony where we hear the call.
With melodies that intertwine,
Our souls dance close, a sacred sign.

The gentle hum of love's sweet song,
In each vibration, we belong.
A chorus sung beneath the stars,
Resonating love, healing scars.

In rhythmic beats, our hearts align,
A gentle touch that feels divine.
We echo laughter, joy, and pain,
In harmonious ties, we remain.

Each note a promise, bold and true,
A legacy of me and you.
Through every discord, we find peace,
In this tempo, our worries cease.

Together we craft a melody,
In perfect tune, just you and me.
In every chorus, the world will see,
The beauty of our harmony.

Flourishing in Shared Light

Beneath the sun, we stand as one,
In warm embrace, our hearts have spun.
Together we bloom, vibrant and free,
In gardens wild, just you and me.

With every glance, the colors shine,
In shared light, our lives entwine.
Through storms we grow, in gentle rain,
Resilience found through joy and pain.

In whispered dreams, our hopes take flight,
As every star ignites the night.
We dance with shadows, chase the skies,
In the freedom of love that never dies.

Like flowers thriving in the dawn,
In every moment, we have drawn.
Our roots entwined in fertile ground,
In shared light, true love is found.

We cultivate the fields we find,
Nurtured by the love that binds.
Flourishing in every hue,
Together we grow, pure and true.

The Route of Our Hearts

On winding roads, our story starts,
Echoes trace the route of our hearts.
With every step, the path unfolds,
Adventures waiting, dreams to hold.

Through valleys low and mountains high,
Together, love, we touch the sky.
With hands held tight, we face the gate,
In unity, we share our fate.

The rustle of leaves, whispers near,
Guiding us on, erasing fear.
With laughter ringing, spirits soar,
With every turn, we seek for more.

In the tapestry of day and night,
We weave our hopes, our futures bright.
Through every challenge, we find our way,
In the route of love, we choose to stay.

So let us wander, free and bold,
In the map of our hearts, stories told.
Through every journey, hand in hand,
Forever together, we take a stand.

A Tapestry of Emotions

In shadows deep where whispers lie,
Colors blend, a silent sigh.
Joy and sorrow weave their threads,
Painting tales where silence spreads.

Laughter dances on the breeze,
While longing sways like ancient trees.
Threads of hope interlace so tight,
Creating warmth in the coldest night.

Secrets shared with tender grace,
Moments etched, time can't erase.
Fragile hearts, they beat as one,
Underneath the same sweet sun.

Memories flutter like paper kites,
Soaring high on starry nights.
In this quilt, each patch defined,
Reflects the journey of the mind.

Each emotion, a brush of fate,
Bound together, never late.
In the tapestry, love stands tall,
A testament to one and all.

The Road to Forever

Beneath the stars, we find our way,
Hand in hand, come what may.
The road ahead, both rough and bright,
Guided softly by the light.

With every step, our dreams unfold,
Whispers of promise, tales of old.
Through valleys low, and mountains high,
Together, love will never die.

Time may challenge, storms may blow,
But in our hearts, a steady glow.
Through every twist, with steadfast grace,
We journey on, in warm embrace.

When shadows fall and doubts arise,
We lift our heads and touch the skies.
For on this road, we find our home,
In every heartbeat, we shall roam.

Forever calls as we stroll on,
Two souls entwined, like dusk and dawn.
Bound by faith, and love's decree,
On this road, it's you and me.

Moonlit Promises

Beneath the moon's soft silver glow,
Promises whispered, hearts aglow.
In shadows deep, we find our dreams,
Where nothing's ever as it seems.

Gentle breezes carry our sighs,
With every glance, our spirits rise.
Stars above bear witness surely,
To vows exchanged so sweetly, purely.

The night enfolds us, wrapped in bliss,
As we share a tender kiss.
Moments pause, time stands still,
In this embrace, we feel the thrill.

Waves of starlight dance on the sea,
A perfect backdrop, just you and me.
Each heartbeat echoes, loud and clear,
In every whisper, you are near.

With the dawn, our dreams may shift,
But moonlit promises, a timeless gift.
As long as stars above remain,
Our love will linger through joy and pain.

In the Garden of Us

In blooms of spring, our laughter found,
A secret garden, love unbound.
Petals soft, in colors bright,
Whispering dreams in morning light.

With every breeze, the flowers sway,
Echoing words we long to say.
Among the vines, our hearts entwine,
In this haven, love will shine.

Butterflies dance with gentle grace,
Reflecting beauty, our sacred space.
Roots run deep, through storm and sun,
In this garden, two become one.

Sunsets paint the sky with fire,
Igniting in us a deep desire.
With every dusk, a promise made,
In this paradise, fears will fade.

Through seasons change, we'll tend the soil,
With every act, the hearts uncoil.
In the garden where love is free,
We blossom ever, you and me.

9 789916 891216